A WORKBOOK IN *THE*

FUNDAMENTALS OF SINGING

by

Frederic Fay Swift

MUS. B., M.S., MUS. D.

Foreword

More people engage in singing than in any other form of musical activity. There are literally millions of singers in our churches, our schools, and our community choirs. Men and women sing regularly in civic and fraternal organizations. Everyone sings.

Each of us has a voice and while some of us will not become professional singers, each of us can learn to sing correctly. Even while reading these words, you may be conscious of some popular tune running through your mind. Each of us sings many times a day and in many different situations.

The fundamentals of singing are not difficult to understand or to master. In school music competitions, it is not uncommon to find that some high school youngster who has never received any "formal" voice training, will receive an "A" rating singing some song which is not too difficult. It is a true statement that some people sing accurately ... naturally. Many of us who get into bad singing habits do so because we imitate poor examples. Entire communities have been known to have poor vocal habits because someone in the community had set a poor example.

Not everyone is endowed with a beautiful voice ... but everyone can learn to use his voice correctly.

In the pages which follow, the fundamentals of singing will be stated in simple language. Children as well as adults can learn to sing correctly. As they mature, they will continue to sing correctly. In time we shall reach a high standard of choral music in our communities and eventually in our country.

A WORKBOOK IN THE FUNDAMENTALS OF SINGING is intended to lay the foundation for voice culture based upon common sense and reason.

(Instead of devoting several pages to songs which might be used, it is recommended that the fundamentals learned here be applied to any singing. Hymns may be used; selections from choir anthems serve as fine exercises. Many people like to sing popular songs ... which may be sung as correctly as any other type of songs. Any choral selection may be used to apply the fundamentals learned in this study.)

E.L. 1254

Table of Contents

We Are All Singers

Singing is probably the oldest form of music art. Much of our speech is based upon singing. As we sustain words . . . and slow up our talking . . . we approach singing. Singing is speaking words on a pitch. Humming is singing without words.

In the ancient past, as singers wished to have an accompaniment for their singing, they began to produce a rhythm, pounding on sticks. This eventually led to playing on drums and hollow logs. In time other instruments were added and bands and orchestras were formed. At first these instruments played the same parts that the voices were singing. A few centuries ago instrumentalists were given other parts to play.

Because each of us is endowed with a voice, singing is universal. We find singing groups in every area of the world. It is natural that we sing. Little children "croon" to themselves as they are learning to talk. In many cases . . . children produce musical tones before they are able to produce words. As children grow up they sing musical games: "London Bridge" and "The Farmer in the Dell". Singing is such a common part of some homes that many children have been able to match pitches (sing the sounds they hear) before they

were a year old. By the time children are two years old they may sing several songs.

If we were to record the number of times that we sing during a day, it would astonish us. We hear a popular song on the radio and a few minutes later we are singing it. Someone whistles a melody . . . and we in turn sing it. In order to speed up the sale of some items, there are singing "commercials". These are catchy tunes which we associate with a certain product. We in turn sing them.

In early history we find that man sang in praise of God. At one time, only the priests were allowed to sing. Songs were sung according to rigid rules. No one was permitted to interfere with the "language of the Gods", which was music. Man had to be careful that he did not offend the gods by "misusing" their language. Later beggars were allowed to sing and by singing their plea for alms, they hoped to receive larger gifts from their listeners.

Music was first introduced into the world several thousands of years ago . . . long before the time of Christ. The majority of this music was vocal.

Questions:

1. Probably the first accompaniment for singing was provided by _____ _____.

2. Some children have been able to match pitches before they were _____ year old.

3. Singing is _____ _____ _____ _____ _____.

4. When we sing without words, we _____.

5. Music was considered the "language of the _____".

History of Singing

Bible records in the Old Testament report on singing for many different occasions. The Jewish people sang to celebrate a victory over their enemies. Music was sung at weddings. It was a part of national activities. Thousands of people sang as a part of their temple worship.

Among the Greeks, long before the time of Christ, thousands of people sang at the music festivals which were held regularly. Greece had its famous singers as well as its statesmen and political leaders.

By the 4th century after Christ's time, The Roman Catholic Church had established its First Singing School. This was sponsored to help train the priests and monks how to sing. Because much of the mass was music, it was necessary to train the Church leaders to sing correctly. We should realize that much of our music notation came from the Church. For a period of over 1000 years, the Church was the dominating music force in the world.

During the Middle Ages singing was limited in great part to the Church program. This followed an earlier tradition that music was a part of religion. However, the "Traveling Singers" of Europe spread the idea that music did not have to be sacred, and people began to sing music outside of the church . . . in their own language. The Minnesingers and Meistersingers were active in Germany. The Troubadours and Trouveres led the movement in France. Many of these were traveling musicians. They entertained the people by traveling from one community to another singing songs in the language of the people. The people, eager to sing, would in turn re-sing the music they had heard from the "traveling singers".

As more people became interested in singing, it was natural that the better singers became teachers. Teachers of 300 or 400 years ago took their pupils into their homes, so that they might live and study together. Lessons were given every day. As the pupils sang, the teachers were able to listen and make corrections when needed. Singers belonged to a "guild" similar to that of carpentry, weaving, or other trades.

During this period the opera and oratorio were developed. Some of the singers of this era were excellent musicians. Their music has come down to us and is standard repertoire for our singers today.

Questions:

1. Name two nations which had singing before the time of Christ. _____, _____.

2. Name 4 different groups of "traveling singers". _____, _____, _____, _____.

3. In what century was the First Singing School started? _____.

4. Why did the Church establish a Singing School? _____ _____ _____ _____.

5. About how long did it take to develop notation? _____ _____ _____.

Singing in America

Singing was very popular in America even before the time of the Revolutionary War. The early Church Fathers of New England brought their own hymns when they came here from the "Old Country". Everyone attended church ... and everyone sang. While we have the names of several of the hymn tunes used at this time, one of them, "Old Hundred" or the "Doxology" is used today. This is indicative of the type of hymns used during this period.

The first book printed in America was the BAY PSALM BOOK ... a hymnbook for church worship. It was printed without notation. (Probably at that time very few people know how to read music.)

Soon after this period, communities where musical interest was high began to hold music festivals. In Bethlehem, Pennsylvania, people gathered together to sing. Singing societies were organized in many cities in the East. In the early 1800's a trained leader, with a suitable number of singing books, arranged a schedule of rehearsals in various communities on a weekly circuit. Traveling from one village to another, he was a Singing Master who directed choirs in several communities. Young and old would attend his singing school, which met in the Town Hall or some other meeting place. Singing became one of the most popular forms of entertainment. Before the days of radio, television, or the movies, singing was one of the more popular forms of amusement.

In 1837, singing was introduced into the schools of Boston. Lowell Mason, the Father of Music Education in our country, started the program which today reaches into the schools in every community of our land. For many years the only music taught in our schools was singing. Boys and girls were taught to read music with facility. Children were able to read "at sight" some of the more difficult selections of the day. Entire schools joined together to sing a cantata or to present a pageant. We have records of "everyone in the school" singing Handel's MESSIAH or Mendelssohn's ELIJAH.

Following World War I, instrumental music was widely introduced into the school program. Today most schools have a fine balance between the vocal and instrumental music programs. Most music students find that they wish to prepare for the instrumental as well as the vocal side of music. As a result we find far better musicians in our school bands, orchestras, and choirs.

Questions:

1. What was the name of the first book printed in America? _____ _____ _____ ____

2. Name one city which started music festivals more than 100 years ago. _____.

3. Who was the founder of music education in America? _____ _____.

4. In what year was music first introduced into the Boston schools? _____.

5. Name one melody which was used in our early American churches and which is sung today.

_____ _____ _____ _____ _____

Vocal Music in Our Schools

When a person plays an instrument in our bands or orchestras, it is naturally assumed that he has received instruction in learning how to play. Not many members of our bands and orchestras are able to play without being taught. In the early days of instrumental music in our schools, lessons were given by a traveling teacher (much like the singing master of the 19th century). Today most schools employ a trained teacher in instrumental music. Students are given lessons privately, or in small groups, so that they may become members of school bands or orchestras.

This is not the case with vocal music. Here singers are admitted to school choirs if they have "sweet voices"; if they are able to sing their own part; and if they are able to blend their voices with others. We accept people who wish to sing, and then trust to luck that we will have enough good singers on each part so that we may have a chorus. A few schools offer classes in SINGING or in VOCAL LESSONS. Many do not. Failure to offer such instruction may be due to several reasons. 1) Insufficient time in the teaching schedule. 2) Lack of interest on the part of the pupils. 3) The chorus may sound quite well without offering such a program so "why offer it?"

While some schools have excellent choirs without offering vocal instruction, the fact remains that many of our young Americans know very little about singing. We have a generation of citizens who like to sing, are eager to sing, but who lack the "know how" to sing. The performance we often accept from our singers, would not be accepted from our instrumentalists. Trained performers on instruments in our communities have set a fine standard of performance. Many communities lack this leadership in choral music.

How can we improve our standards? The answer is quite simple. As an instrumentalist is trained in the proper way to play; as he is given instruction in proper tone quality, articulation and technic, so the vocal student should be trained in the fundamentals of singing.

If time cannot be found in the schedule to allow the vocal teacher to give private or class lessons (and if time is found for instrumental music it should also be provided for choral music), then the teacher must train the singers during the choir rehearsal. As we have class lessons for various combinations of instrumentalists, so we must apply the same principle to the chorus.

The means of improving our American standards of singing is found in our public schools.

Questions:

1. Instrumental lessons may be given privately or in _____.

2. American standards depend upon the program taught in our _____.

3. Name 3 requirements for admission to a school choir. _____, _____, _____.

4. Is it possible that a school might have a good choir and the singers not know very much about correct singing?

_____

5. Standards of instrumental and vocal performance are similar. _____.

LESSON 5

Our Singing Instrument

Acoustics is the science of sound. While the human voice differs from all other instruments, and each voice is different from all others, it must, none the less, follow certain acoustical laws. In order to produce sound, something must vibrate. In the case of the voice, sound is produced by the vibration of the vocal cords. Although these are called vocal cords, they are NOT strings like those on a violin. Our voice is not a stringed instrument. Rather ... because our tones are produced by breath ... we might say that our voice is a wind instrument.

Breath passing over (between) the vocal cords, sets them into vibration. The tone formed is reenforced in our chest, mouth and head cavities thereby the tone is amplified. By the use of our tongue, lips, teeth, and other organs of speech ... we add words.

But singing is not entirely physical.... There are several things which we do "with our minds" when we sing.

Mental

There is much more to singing than merely opening our mouths and allowing a sound to come out. Before we make a sound, we have to have some idea in our minds of the way it will sound. We are so built that we merely need to hear a sound and we are able immediately to produce the same pitch with our voice. (Providing of course that it is within our range.) Most people are able to do this. A few people cannot. Practically everyone can be taught to sing in tune ... if they wish to do so ... and if they are willing to spend the time to do so. If we write the word PUESSITUDE (a word which has no meaning as far as we know) ... someone reads it ... speaks the word aloud ...and immediately everyone in our class can repeat it. We repeat it because "in our minds we have heard the way it should sound." A similar happening occurs when we sing. Almost automatically we think a pitch and sing it. When we read music we see a note which represents a tone in our minds. We then sing the pitch which we "think it is".

Besides this mental experience in singing, we also must have a desire to sing (also mental), we must think of the interpretation we shall give the song, and the quality of voice we shall use in singing. Several of these shall be further discussed in the next lesson.

Questions:

1. The science of sound is named _____.

2. Tones are reenforced in our _____, _____, and _____.

3. 4. 5. Name 3 mental activities when we sing.

_____ _____ _____.

_____ _____ _____.

_____ _____ _____.

Why People Sing

In order to sing our best, we must WANT to sing. In school, we cannot make boys and girls sing unless they wish to do so. The successful teacher tries to get the students to "want to sing". This is known as motivation. Once the student has found that singing is fun, he will want to sing "for the rest of his life."

In Kiwanis, Rotary, Lion's Club or other service organizations, men sing because it is a fine social experience. It makes us "feel together" when we sing together. Some people do not sing because they do not feel that they have good voices ... however, once this barrier is broken down, everyone sings and enjoys singing together.

It is our belief that just about everyone can sing. There are some individuals who have physical defects which may hamper their singing ... yet even these people can sing a little. Perhaps they have a limited range ... or do not have good quality, it is still their contribution to the world of music. In a way ... the entire world is ONE HUMAN VOICE ... the voice of humanity. Our voice enters this picture at our lowest tone and continues to our highest. Other voices sing lower, and still other voices sing higher. Yet each voice has a place in the total picture of mankind singing.

We discover that certain moods bring out the desire to sing. When we are all pepped up we feel like singing. Taking a shower makes us want to sing. A bright day and a clear sky makes us want to sing. Happiness makes us eager to sing. We in turn sing to show others that we are happy. At athletic events we stand with our classmates and sing our Alma Mater. We are proud of our school ... and we express this pride in singing.

In our homes we sing. It unites the members of the family to sing together. Driving along in cars ... we sing. We may turn on the radio and sing with the artist who is entertaining us. While we are dancing ... we are softly singing.

While we have been discussing singing aloud, much of our singing is done "in our minds". We THINK through a song many times before we sing it aloud. One famous teacher suggested that much of singing practice should be "silently done". We interpret the song the way we "FEEL" it should be sung. Because our voice is US, we sing as WE feel ... This gives us "self expression" ... and this is one of the most important phases of any form of art.

Questions:

Answer true or false to the following.

1. Only a few individuals are singers and not everyone can sing. _____

2. Happiness makes us eager to sing. _____

3. Singing should be fun. _____

4. All singing should be aloud . _____

5. Self expression is one of the most important reasons that people sing. _____

LESSON 7

Breathing

The first fundamental of singing is breath support.

Many pages have been written on how we should breathe when we sing. In our thinking together about breathing, we are going to give a few suggestions and not try to cover all of the details.

In order to breathe correctly, the singer sits erect (not rigid) or stands erect. We must be erect because in this position the muscles of the diaphragm and ribs can most easily do their work. We lean away from the back of the chair so that it is easier to breathe ... we are alert.

People breathe without thinking about it. While we sleep, we breathe. This is involuntary breathing. We breathe without being conscious of it. However, by thinking about it, we can take a breath when we wish. This is voluntary breathing. When we sing, we control our breathing, deciding when to take a breath and when not to take a breath. As we become proficient singers, we breathe where the music allows us to do so.

The fact that we have been breathing normally for a number of years, does not mean that we breathe correctly for singing. Some people do breathe correctly, and probably this number is greater than we might expect. However, whether or not we breathe correctly, we should study the various statements made about breath control.

At this point it might be well to express an opinion or two on the entire process of singing. We might spend a considerable amount of time learning the names of the organs of the body which are used in singing, and then learning how each functions. Still, knowing this might not help us in any way toward our goal of becoming a good singer. It is our purpose to give a program of proper singing . . . and only as far as it is necessary, will we give details on the actions of these

are to have good tone quality, we must have good breath support. If we wish to sing in tune, we must have proper breathing. If we wish to interpret the music, singing it phrase by phrase as the composer intended, we must rely on our breathing to sustain it.

_____ d all singing. If we

is _____ _____

_____ nd erect when we sing.

_____ _____ _____.

_____ out it it is called _____ _____.

_____ for singing without having studied how to do so? _____

_____ names and functions of the body organs used in singing before we can become good

LESSON 8

Suggestions on Breathing

Our lungs are located in our chest cavities. It is from the lungs that breath is exhaled and passed over the vocal cords to produce tones. The following statements apply to the kind of breathing used with singing.

1. We take a breath through the nose and the mouth. We don't inhale through the nose alone . . . it takes too long.
2. We should take a breath inaudibly (without anyone hearing it).
3. With the mouth slightly open we are able to take a breath in a fraction of a second (almost a gasp breath).
4. When we breathe in (inhale) the diaphragm pulls down, the intercostal muscles force the chest out, and air rushes into the lungs.
5. Having inhaled the breath correctly does not presuppose that we will exhale it correctly.

singing . . . otherwise the muscles are moving against the chair).
7. About 70% of our breathing is done with the diaphragm, 30% with the intercostal muscles.
8. We expand as we breathe. We do not breathe to expand.
9. We may do breathing exercises if we wish to acquire more breath. When we exercise, our diaphragms are moving more often and we are taking deeper breaths.
10. Panting may be used as a breathing exercise, but don't do it too long or you will get dizzy.
11. Sniffing is a good exercise. Imagine that you are smelling a rose. Take several sniffs on the same inhale. (You may be able to take 20 or 30 sniffs on one long inhale.) Actually the diaphragm pulls down . . . the air rushes in . . . then the diaphragm pulls down again. This is allowing you to control the diaphragm.

The above statements apply to inhaling. It is necessary to have a good supply of breath in order to sing long phrases. Shorter phrases will require less breath.

_____.

_____.

_____ or false:

_____.

_____ ne with the diaphragm.

c. Intercostal muscles are found between the ribs. _____.

d. When we sing we breathe only through the nose. _____.

4. Name two exercises which improve our ability to inhale. _____, _____.

Exhaling

Assuming that we have a normal supply of breath in our lungs, we must now consider what happens when we exhale.

We do not need more breath than we are going to use in the singing of the phrase before us. In this respect, we have to plan ahead as to the amount of breath we shall need.

Here are some suggestions for exhalation:

1. The air passing from the lungs, through the trachea and over the vocal cords, sets them into vibration. This produces a tone.
2. Do not try to hold the chest up as you exhale. When you inhaled, the intercostal muscles expanded and the chest expanded. Now that you are exhaling, the chest returns to a normal position; the space becomes smaller.
3. Many people use too much of the breath on the first few tones of the phrase. Plan ahead and save your breath, so that you will have enough for the final tones of the phrase.
4. As you sing higher, you need more support. The singer will notice that the diaphragm tightens more as the air is forced up with greater force. (The diaphragm is a thin muscular partition, separating the chest cavity from the abdominal cavity.) We are able to produce high tones more easily by greater support rather than by tightening of the throat.
5. A fine exercise for exhaling is the issuing of a steady flow of breath from the mouth while the lips are in the position of a small OOH. Proceed from this by adding a soft tone on an OOH.
6. With a little practice, singers will find that the body relaxes and the chest gradually subsides as the breath is used.
7. Even young singers are able to sustain a tone softly for 15 seconds or more. (This, by the way, is about as long a phrase as most young singers are required to sing.)

By observing the length of the phrase to be sung, and by planning ahead, the young singer will be able to estimate the amount of breath he will need. Taking too deep a breath is harmful to the singer. The muscles are expanded as far as possible, tending to produce rigidity.

Many of our singing faults are traced to poor breathing. As we continue our study we shall mention breath support on many occasions. A person does not become 100% proficient with breathing before moving on to other phases of singing. Good breath support is brought about gradually and over a long period of time.

Questions:

1. When we sing, what vibrates to produce a tone? _____.

2. Many people use too much breath at the _____ of a phrase.

3. A young singer should be able to sustain a tone for _____ seconds.

4. Is it true that as we exhale the chest remains high? _____.

5. Why is it harmful to take too deep a breath? _____ _____ _____.

Producing Tones

Breath passing over the vocal cords produces tones. If we were to place our hands on our throats as we sang, we would feel the movement. Our larynx, located about halfway between the chin and the chest, is the organ which contains the vocal cords.

One of the marvels of the world of acoustics lies in the fact that this small larynx can produce such a variety of tones. A man will sing low sounds, which can only be imitated by large bass horns, yet the sounds are made by this small instrument in his throat. Recent scientific studies have helped to explain this.

A little more than a century ago, man invented a laryngoscope. This was an instrument with mirrors which would permit a doctor to look into a person's throat while he was singing. Man could then see what was happening during the production of a singing tone.

Vocal cords are not cords at all, but are membranes or muscles which extend from the sides of the larynx. On low tones these membranes are held back against the sides, and a large column of breath moves between them. They vibrate slowly. As the pitch goes higher the membranes move out across the air passage. They even touch each other until the size of the opening between them is very small. The vocal cords also thin or thicken within themselves.

While this information is interesting, it does little to help us sing correctly.

Basically, we have to depend on our ears to guide us to the proper pitch and the best tone quality of which we are capable. In improving our tones there are two basic types of exercise which we may use. The first is the use of the sustained tone; the second, the short detached or staccato tone.

In the latter type, the breath is taken between tones. During this the vocal cords return to their "at ease" position. Then they move out to the proper position (approximate) for the pitch to be produced.

In the lesson which follows we are going to sing some exercises dealing with the points discussed till now.

Questions:

1. What is the name of the instrument which allows us to study the throat as someone is singing? _____

2. Vocal cords are _____ or _____.

3. Vocal cords are found in the _____.

4. Name two exercises which help us improve our vibrating organs. _____ and _____.

5. When we take a breath, the vocal cords return to the _____ _____ position.

Vibrating Exercises

Let us sing the following exercises on the vowel sound AH. In the first we shall sustain the tone as long as it is needed. In the second, we shall take a breath between each tone.... It is not our purpose to make beautiful sounds at this time ... merely to experiment with our vibrating organs.

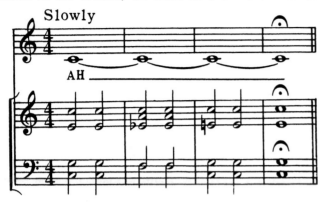

Sing slowly and take a breath between each tone.

Continue exercise in following keys.

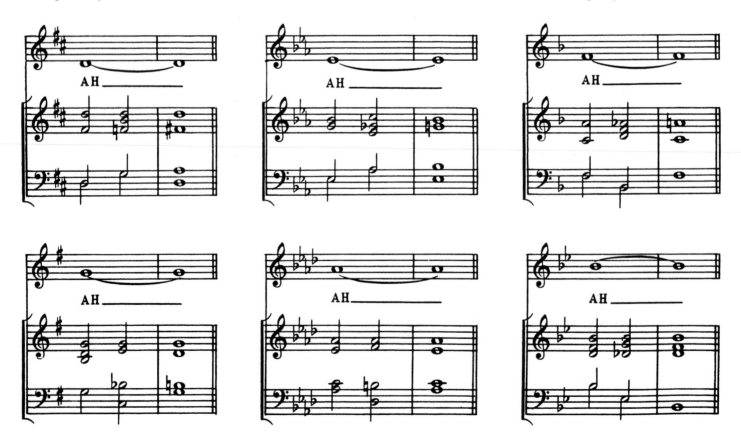

Some Warnings

While most of us are able to sing without fear of injuring our voices, there are occasions when it is wiser that we do not sing.

People who are suffering from a sore throat, or from a cold in the throat, may find it irritating to try and sing. When a person has laryngitis, it is not good to sing. Don't do anything which will prevent the throat from becoming normal as soon as possible.

One of the finest of "relaxers" for our throats is yawning. If singers have been singing for a long period of time, the throat muscles become tired. Rest a while

...yawn...and try to keep that relaxed feeling.

As the young singer learns to sing correctly, he will be able to sing for an hour or two at a time. However, there is little merit in trying to force one's voice by singing too long. Sing easily. Let the breath support the tone. Do not strain for high notes. Do not sing too loudly. Straining is often done in the throat, and the throaty quality of a singer who is forcing his voice is unpleasant to the listener.

Sing the following exercises easily...good breath support....

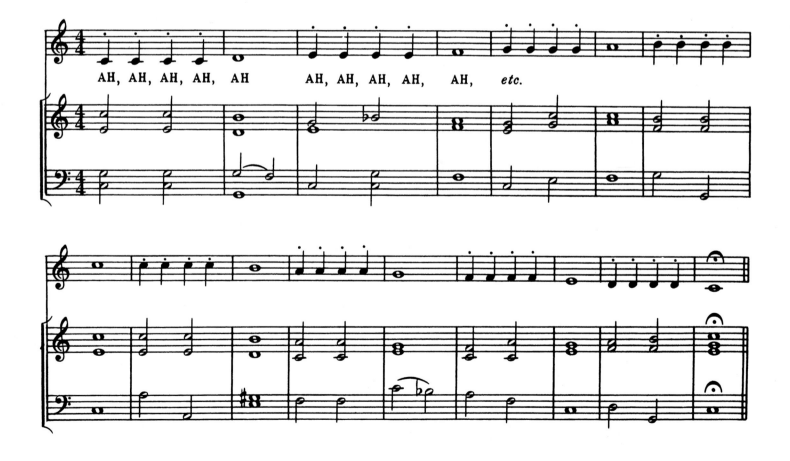

Speech and Singing

We have learned that singing is speaking on a tone. It is natural to assume that many of the things we learn about singing will also apply to our speaking voices. For a few minutes let us compare and contrast our singing and speaking habits.

While we speak, vowels and consonants come together very rapidly. We may say a sentence at any speed we wish, dwell on some words or syllables as we may prefer, yet we usually complete the thought with one breath. In singing we usually speak consonants quickly. We sustain the vowel sounds as long as the music requires, and we take a breath where the music indicates that we may. In singing, the consonants provide the skeleton of the words and the vowel sounds fill in between.

As we shall see in our study of vowel sounds, about the only sounds we can sustain (in any language) are vowel sounds. If we try and sustain the sound of the second letter of the alphabet "B", we have an explosion of the lips ... and then the sound we sustain is an EEH. The same is true of most consonants. In speech we do not worry about this. In singing, we are ever conscious of the vowel sounds which we are sustaining. The singing of vowels correctly is one of the first marks of a trained singer.

In our singing and in our speech, the physical, mental, and emotional conditions unite to give us the quality which is US. The person who feels ill, reflects this fact in his speech as well as in his singing.

Both speech and singing are based upon breath support. Listen to some of the fine actors on radio and television, or on the stage. Notice how they project their words by fine breath support. Many such individuals study voice so that they may carry over from singing some of the fundamentals necessary in good speaking.

Because singing requires more thought and concentration than does speech, it follows that if we learn to sing correctly, it will aid us in our speaking habits. To enunciate clearly and to pronounce accurately will aid us as singers. It will also be reflected in our speaking voices. As we enter the lessons on correct singing, try and apply them to your everyday speaking.

Questions:

1. In singing we sustain _____.

2. In singing, the consonants form the _____ of the words.

3. Is it true that our physical, mental, and emotional feelings are shown in both our singing and speaking voices?

_____

4. Both speech and singing are based upon _____ _____.

5. Which requires more thought and concentration: speaking or singing? _____.

Vowel Sounds

Our alphabet is composed of vowels and consonants. Vowels are the letters A, E, I, O, U, and sometimes W and Y. Actually there are five vowel *sounds* in our singing even though we may have more than 5 letters of the alphabet called vowels. The vowel sounds are AYE, EEH, AH, OH, and OOH.

As we look at these vowel sounds, we notice that AH is located in the center. This is the most normal of all sounds which we make. Most children speak their first word on an AH. They say Ma, Ma, or Da, Da. If we hum and open our lips with our fingers ... we hear a series of Ma, Ma's. (Try it.)

AYE and EEH are called bright vowels. When we sing them, our lips are pulled apart. The sounds come "through our teeth". We tend to smile as we sing them.

OH and OOH are called dark vowels. We cover our teeth with our lips when we sing these vowel sounds. We move our lips forward on OH and even more forward closing the opening for OOH.

From the first attempt at singing correctly, we must establish in our own minds the mouth position we have when we sing EACH of these vowel sounds. There may be some slight difference between the mouth position we have and that of some other singer ... but each of us must realize that there is a distinct position for our tongue, lips, teeth ... when we sing each of these sounds. It may aid us if we look in a mirror as we sing these sounds. Listen to make sure that we have the finest sound on the vowel that we can make. Our mouths must be open to let the tones out. Sing AH ... open the mouth a little more and see if it improves the tone. Find the position which sounds best to YOU.

Now sing AYE ... notice how we close our mouth a little. Now change to an EEH and notice that we close our mouth still more. Try adding a smile as you sing EEH. Does it change the quality?

When we change from an AH to an OH . . . notice how we move our lips out . . . and when we sing on OOH, we move them still further. While singing OOH . . . move the lips still farther forward and notice the quality change.

WHILE WE ARE SINGING ANY ONE VOWEL SOUND, WE MUST NOT MOVE OUR MOUTH. If we do so, we will get another vowel sound. This is extremely important. Think it through. As soon as we have mastered this fact, we are well on our way to pronouncing correctly when we sing. Many of our popular singers break this rule all of the time. Watch them on TV or in a concert appearance. It is so simple if we will do the proper thing. One cannot produce the same vowel sound with two different mouth positions . . . it is impossible . . . and to sing the wrong vowel sound is vocally wrong.

Questions:

1. Name the dark vowel sounds. _____ and _____ .

2. Name the bright vowel sounds. _____ and _____ .

3. Which is the easiest vowel sound to make? _____ .

4. Why should we not change our mouth positions while singing a single vowel sound?

_____ _____ _____ _____ _____ _____ _____

5. How many primary vowel sounds do we have in our language? _____ .

LESSON 15

Singing Vowels

Not everyone will have exactly the same mouth positions for the same vowel sounds. In some areas of our country, there are differences in pronunciation. In the South, we have a "softer" quality of speech. In some areas of the North, the speech is "sharper" . . . crisper in quality. Within our voice there is a "best position for us." All people will have similar positions . . . mouth, tongue, lips, teeth . . . for the same vowel sounds.

Shown below are some pictures showing correct mouth positions for our 5 primary vowel sounds.

EEH

AYE

AH

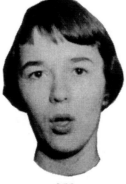

OH

OOH

Vocalizing Vowels

As we have stated, AH is the most natural of sounds for us to make. Because of this, we shall start our vocalizing with this vowel sound. We must remember that we do not change our vowel position when we sing higher or lower . . . that is done with the breath support and the vocal cords. We are not trying to sing high or low . . . we are trying to get the correct sound when we sing AH.

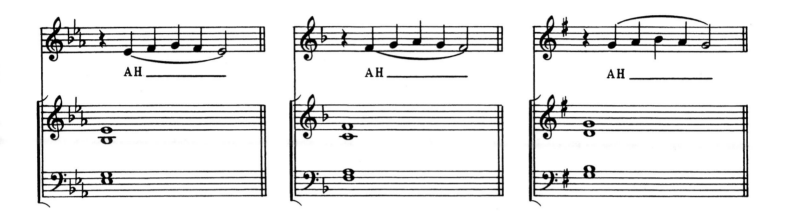

Continue the exercise to A-flat, and B-flat. From B-flat return downward singing A-flat, G, F, and E-flat.

Let us now repeat the exercise singing on the other vowel sounds. OH, OOH, AYE and EEH. Remember that in each case the vowel sound has a definite mouth position. We make this position and sing on it. In every case, we try and make the best AH, AYE, EEH, OH and OOH that we can.

Below are some additional exercises for us to sing.

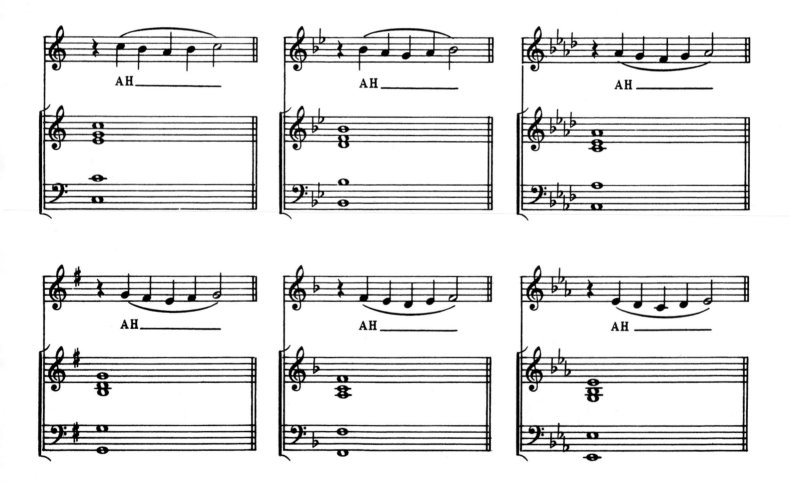

Vowel Sounds of Songs

In this lesson we are going to sing familiar songs using vowel sounds only. There will not be any words . . . only vowels. As you sing . . . be sure to change to the correct vowel sound at the right time.

AMERICA

TELL ME WHY!

E.L. 1254

More Vowel Sounds

The common vowels in our alphabet are A, E, I, O, U. The prime vowels of our language are AYE, EEH, AH, OH, OOH. These are not identically the same. We have two sounds for "A" ... AYE and AH ... and we do not have a prime sound for "I".

This leads us to realize that there are more vowel sounds than the five prime sounds we have learned. The sound for "I" is a combination of AH and EEH. We sing most of the time value on AH and then just before we move on to the next sound, we change the mouth to form the EEH. The combination of the two gives us the "I" sound.

We also should realize that there are several pronunciations of the alphabet vowels, many of them sounding like other singing vowels. For example ... the "I" in the word MACHINE ... is pronounced like an "E" ... EEH. The "O" in NOT is pronounced like an AH.

Some of these sounds are slightly "between" the prime vowel sounds ... others are a combination of vowels.

In the words which follow, we have tried to give the more common vowels and the different pronunciations which we must recognize. Each of the following is a little different than the others.
A—Fate, fare, fat, far, fast.
E—Fear, fed.
I—Find, fill.
O—Fold, fort, fog, food, foot.
U—Flute, fun.

Undoubtedly there are people who will recognize a fine difference between other words in our language. Most of us will recognize differences in each of these.

As we have learned in this lesson, not all vowels are the pure sounds of AYE, EEH, AH, OH, and OOH ... a few are slight modifications of these ... the mouth may be in a position between two of these prime vowels. Yet in every case, there is a position for US which gives us the best sounding vowel we can produce. This we find and this we use when we sing.

Questions:

1. Which of the alphabet vowels is a combination of two singing vowels? _____

2. Which of the "O" vowels sound like a "U"? _____

3. Name word with an "O" vowel which sounds like an AH. _____

4. What is a word showing a short "E" sound? _____

5. What is a word showing the long "E" sound? _____

(We should notice that we have a long and a short vowel sound for each of the vowels.)

Write intervals

Singing Words

Now that we have learned about the many vowel sounds, we are going to sing them. As yet we have not discussed consonants and in this lesson we are not trying to sing them correctly ... however ... we wish to point out that WE SING ON THE VOWELS ... the con-sonants before and after vowels will take only a moment of our time. As we sang vowels in lessons 16 and 17, continue to sing them in this lesson. Merely pronounce the consonants as quickly as possible ... SING THE VOWELS.

SWEET AND LOW

Diphthongs

In our previous lesson we learned that there are vowel sounds in addition to the five prime vowels we have already studied. Some of these use mouth positions which are "between" the five prime vowels.

We may have already noticed that some words have two vowels located together. These are called diphthongs. When we speak these words we find that we must articulate both vowels.

Vowels have a way of moving from one to another very freely. In singing we would say "The boy ate THEE apple." Because apple begins with a vowel sound, we say THEE and our tone then flows uninterruptedly into the next word.

There are many English words with diphthongs. A few examples are: house, boil, view, beauty, etc.

It is impossible for us to give a series of rules which we follow in singing diphthongs. In speech, when words move swiftly, we do not need to concentrate on these. In singing, when a definite amount of time is given each vowel sound, we have to be more accurate. When singing a diphthong we often give the first vowel sound the greater amount of time value. If we sing the word "Joy," we sing the "O" sound for almost all of the time value allotted it . . . in a fraction of a second we add the "Y" sound.

In the word "few" we reverse this policy. We hardly pronounce the "E" sound . . . we sustain the "W" sound . . . OOH.

In order to be assured of singing correctly, the singer should consult a dictionary. We must remember that in singing the words take precedence over the music. We speak correctly when we sing. Singing is speaking on a tone. We do not wish to have our singing so poor that no one understands us. We should never sing "songs without words" . . . unless we are humming.

In the exercise below . . . we have tried to show how we treat diphthongs.

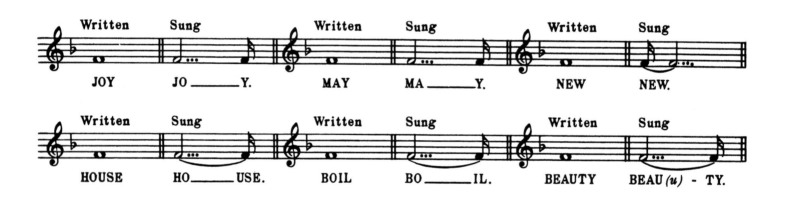

Consonants

While there are many more letters of the alphabet which are consonants than there are vowels, we do not spend as much time with them as we do with the vowel sounds. As we have learned, sustained tones are made up of vowel sounds. Consonants are spoken before or after vowels to form the words.

In a way we may divide all consonants into three types. 1—Those formed with the lips, 2—those formed with the teeth, and 3—those which in a small way may be held out and may become a part of the sustained tone like vowels.

Listed below we are giving the letters of the alphabet and we shall then classify them as type 1, 2, or 3.

B—1	C—2	D—2	F—1	G—2	H—2
J—2	K—2	L—3	M—3	N—3	P—1
Q—1	R—2	S—2	T—2	W—1	X—2
Y—	Z—2				

We will notice that those marked with letter 3 may be held out. The sounds of L, M, and N may be held out. On the "L" sound, the tongue moves up to the roof of the mouth and the tone continues to come out of our mouths. In the case of the sounds of "M" and "N" . . . we may close our mouths and the tone will continue to come out of our nose. If we hold our nose . . . the tone will stop.

In recent years, vocalists have achieved some very fine effects with the use of hums and "L" sounds. We may hum with our mouths open and our tongues against the roof of our mouths similar to the "L" sound. We may hum with our mouths open and our lips closed over our teeth. This gives a very fine effect. (Leave your lips closed and bring your jaws apart.) However, we should point out here that this type of singing does NOT belong in a song of the old masters. If we are to sing the music of the classical or romantic composers, we should sing it in the style which the composers intended. Modern music of the semi-serious variety is often sung with the hum and other choral effects.

Questions:

1. Name two consonants which we form with our lips. _____, _____.

2. Name two consonants which we may prolong. _____, _____.

3. Name two consonants which are formed by the teeth. _____, _____.

4. Consonants are spoken _____ or _____ vowels to sound words.

5. When we sing an "L" sound, does the sound come out of our mouths or out of our noses? _____.

Singing Consonants

In the previous lesson we learned that consonants are formed with our lips and teeth. In other words . . . the greater emphasis for the sounds are directed toward the lips or teeth. Actually there is more than this in singing consonants.

With some consonants, we allow the tone to continue . . . the "S" sound in sing, smoke, or smile . . . is prolonged longer than many other consonant tones. To prolong an "S" sound we have a hiss . . . yet it may be prolonged. The sound of "TH" may be sustained. "F" prolonged. The sound of "TH" may be sustained. "F" may be held out . . . as can "R".

On the other hand, we have some consonants which

seem to stop the breath (and the tone) and then explode the sound. Take for instance the letter "P" or "B".

We point these out because we wish each reader to be conscious of the many points of clear enunciation which one must consider. It is impossible to give rules for the correct pronunciation of every consonant . . . and it is not our purpose to do so . . . however, each singer has to think of these things and be as accurate as he can when singing.

In the words which we have for the exercise . . . note how some of the consonants "explode" . . . others only partially stop the breath.

Continue the exercise singing . . .

Do, Doo, Daye, etc.

Ho, Hoo, Haye, etc.

Go, Goo, Gaye, etc.

To, Too, Taye, etc.

Use other consonants.

More Consonants

We find that there are several words which use double vowels (diphthongs). It is also true that there are a great many words which use double consonants. As we stated before, our own ears will have to be the judge as to how best to pronounce such words. In many cases each consonant is heard. In other cases the second consonant is lost in the first.

In the word "fumble" . . . we hear the hum on the "M" and again the "ble" sounds. In "Fast" . . . we hear the "S" and the "T" sound. So we might continue with several similar words.

However, in the word "bell" we sound only the one "L". But in a word like "bellows" we sound both "L's".

The consonant "X" is a combination of two other consonant sounds, "K" and "S" . . . and the same consonant "X" sounds like a "Z" in the word "exact".

As we speak the following words, let us be certain that we pronounce the entire word. They have been presented by syllables:

ac-cep-ta-tion; ac-cess; ad-just-ment; af-fair; ag-gra-vate; al-le-lu-ia; an-nex; ap-point; ar-rest; ar-ro-gant; as-sets; at-tic; ax-il; ax-is;

Az-tec; bab-ble; bag-gy; bal-loon; bar-rel; bar-ri-er; bas-sin-et; bat-tery; ba-zoo-ka; bed-ding; bel-low; Bi-ble; etc.

Select words from any dictionary . . . pronounce them correctly. Take notice of the many people about you who do NOT enunciate distinctly. If we are to sing correctly we must pronounce each consonant (as well as each vowel) accurately.

As we have stated before, the pronunciation of certain words differs according to the area from which the speaker comes. Older people sometimes have different pronunciations than do young people. Those who have been reared in foreign lands will have "accents" . . . they speak with a different conception of the way words should sound.

We do not propose that everyone should speak the same . . . but each of us can and should speak correctly. At the same time we will hold to our own individual taste. Some speech experts have spoken of the American people as "slovenly speakers." Perhaps the statement is true. If each of us becomes conscious of the way we pronounce words, we can overcome this fault.

---

1. Name one word which uses a double consonant, and in which the second consonant is not heard. _____.

2. Name a word in which a consonant sounds like two consonants. _____.

3. What is "our judge" for speaking correctly? _____ _____.

4. If we are to sing correctly, we must _____, _____ _____ _____ correctly.

5. Should everyone speak the same? _____.

Pronunciation

In this and the following lesson we are going to apply the facts we have already learned about singing. We are going to sing one of the most standard of hymn tunes...FAITH OF OUR FATHERS.

1. We shall sing it through on the VOWEL SOUNDS ALONE. Do not sing any consonants.

2. Sing the words. BE SURE TO GIVE "ALMOST" ALL OF THE TIME ALLOTTED TO EACH SYLLABLE...TO THE VOWEL SOUND.

3. Check for the suggestions we are giving at various places in the hymn.

FAITH OF OUR FATHERS

A. Sing on the AH sound for 2 beats and then as you are leaving for next syllable (ers) add the "TH" sound.

B. The same here...two beats on the vowel sound ...then add the "ing."

C. Sing the vowel for almost all of the 3 beats, then add the "ll."

D. One syllable...there are NOT two syllables in FIRE.

E. Sing on the vowel OH full beats then add the "rd".

F. Same as A above.

Diction

Diction may be defined in one way as "the art or manner of speaking or singing." We will refer to diction as to the way we speak our vowels, consonants, syllables, words, and phrases. In singing the problem of proper diction is much more difficult than in speaking.

In singing we have to speak the correct syllable (vowel and consonant) at the proper time . . . for the proper duration of time . . . on the correct pitch. Singing is a combination of both speech and tone . . . one must hear the proper word on the proper pitch at the proper time. We do not wish to hear words without tone and we do not wish to hear tones without words. Each must complement the other.

The old Italian school of teachers coined a phrase which every young singer should follow. "The softer we sing, the louder we seem to pronounce." In other words, even when we sing softly, the words are of great importance and should be heard. We must stress words so that our listeners (as well as ourselves) will hear them. Sometimes this is not easy. When we sing very high (or very low) some words are difficult to sing. Most singers discover that the dark vowels (OH and OOH) are best sung on low tones. The bright vowels (EEH and AYE) are easier on high tones. Songs which locate the proper vowels in the proper places greatly aid the singer. Songs with vowels placed indiscriminately in relation to the melody, are difficult to sing.

It is equally difficult to speak all consonants on high or low pitches. In the middle range of our voices, we should be able to speak any words. On our highest and lowest tones this is most difficult.

As young singers, we should select songs which are within our range. There is no great reward for singing something which goes beyond our normal singing voices. It is a common occurrence in our music festivals to hear young singers with very fine voices do miserable performances because the songs they have chosen are beyond their range. A well-known, standard solo, may be purchased in any one of several different keys. The purpose in providing the solo in different keys is to allow the singer to select a key which "fits his voice". In the proper range, most of us are capable of fine diction . . . so it behooves each of us to select a song which fits our voice and which will permit us to sing accurately without forcing the tones.

Questions:

1. Diction is the art or manner of _____ _____ _____.

2. What do we mean by the statement, "The softer we sing the louder we seem to pronounce."

_____ _____

3. Which is of greater importance, the words or the music? _____ · _____ _____ _____

4. Name two vowel sounds that are generally considered easy to sing on high tones.

_____ and _____.

5. Which are easier to sing on low tones, dark or bright vowel sounds? _____.

Vocalizing

Before an instrumentalist plays, he usually "warms up" by playing a series of scales or exercises. He plays tones in the middle range of his instrument. He then plays up and down the scale. He adjusts his lips and fingers to the instrument which he is playing. In some ways singers do the same thing.

When we are members of some choirs the director will spend a few minutes in singing "warming up exercises". Other choir directors use the first song as a "warming up number".

When we sing alone, it is wise to warm up on an exercise called a vocalize. This may be a series of scales or arpeggios based on chords. The purpose of the warming-up exercise is to get our vocal organs limbered up. We get the "frogs out of our throats". We get in the mood to sing. We do some breathing exercises to start us "expanding to sing." After a few moments of exercises, we are ready to sing.

Students of voice use vocalizes as the instrumentalist uses technical studies. Through vocalizing we develop technic. Because of the importance of vocalizing, we shall devote three lessons to it.

In the first place, each singer should wish to extend his range. He should, through the years, be able to sing tones lower and higher than when he started. Too often singers wish to sing only high tones. In such cases, the lower side of the voice may be completely neglected. Each of us has been given a voice to use. By proper training, we should extend the range of this instrument to higher and lower tones.

In recent years the voices of our American popular singers have become noticeably lower. As we listen to several of our radio and television singers, we realize that they are singing songs which go many times below the notes on the treble staff. Through the use of microphones the volume of these tones is built up so that when the sound reaches us in our homes they sound adequate. Young singers should not limit their singing to either "direction". Increase your range both ways.

Besides helping us to extend our singing range, vocalizes aid us in developing greater speed and agility. Other vocalizes (as we have seen) improve our voice quality.

In lesson 27 we are listing exercises that might aid us in extending our range. Notice that on high tones we need fine breath support. We sing staccato exercises. When we sing low tones, we do quite the opposite. We sing softly on sustained tones. Over a few months daily practice we are able to extend the range of our voices. As some songs require quite a wide range, by increasing the tones which we are able to sing, we may embark upon a whole new world of music.

Questions:

1. Name 2 ways a choir may "warm up". _____ _____ _____.

2. Name 2 reasons for "warming up" our voices. _____ _____, _____ _____.

3. Should we extend our range both upwards and downwards? _____.

4. Name two results of vocalizing in addition to increasing our range.

_____ _____, _____ _____ _____ _____ _____.

5. Do we sing staccato or legato exercise to vocalize high tones? _____.

Vocalizing Upward

Most of us like to vocalize with piano accompaniment. This is good because it helps us to "sing in tune". Later when we sing in choirs and are working for a "blend" we often sing unaccompanied (a cappella).

In the exercises which follow, we have arpeggios moving up the scale. Do not force your voice. Give good breath support . . . sing short tones. . . . You will find that you will be able to vocalize to higher tones than you would ordinarily want to sing. By singing staccato tones we increase our range. We sing tones we might not wish to sing if we sustained them.

Continue with other vowel sounds . . . with other consonants preceding them. For example . . . Too, Too, Too, . . . Mo, Mo, Mo, . . . Moo, Moo, Moo, . . . Lah, Lah, Lah, . . . etc.

We practice these and other exercises each day.

Vocalizing Downward

The exercise which we will use in this lesson will be sustained . . . sung slowly . . . in each case we will try to get the best quality we can on the low tones. We relax and sing!

Besides singing with AH, we will also sing with each of the other prime vowels . . . AYE, EEH, OH, AND OOH.

Vocalizes which combine words with these vowel sounds are as follows:

Far the bar.
Cool the moon.

Deep the sea.

Row the boat.
Weigh the gate.

Sing 3 tones on the first word, then one tone each on the other words.

Voice Classification

Heretofore we have not discussed the various classifications of voices. Actually . . . any voice, no matter what the classification, should sing using the fundamentals we have discussed. Each voice should be used correctly, and each singer will find that there are songs published within the range where he sings best.

Until they reach their early teens, practically all children's voices sound similar. While the child may learn to sing the soprano or the alto part, the quality of the voice is about the same. It is like a violin playing similar parts. About the time that children reach junior high school, a difference in quality will be noticed.

In the early teens, the boy's voice changes. It goes lower. It may change suddenly . . . in a few days time . . . or it may change gradually over a longer period of time. Some European teachers recommend that the boy continue to sing "as high as he can" until there is a break in his voice. He then does not sing for a period of time until his voice has "settled" to its permanent range. Most educators in America take an opposite view. We believe that the boy should sing, using the low tones in his range, and, as his voice drops lower and lower, he continues to sing music within his range. He may start as a soprano, then sing alto parts, then alto-tenor parts, and eventually tenor or baritone.

As adult singers (from senior high school on), we have four major classifications of voices. There are smaller subdivisions within these major classifications. The girls' voices are called soprano and alto. The male voices are called tenor, baritone, or bass. (In four parts—soprano, alto, tenor, and baritone.)

There are two major factors to be considered in the classification of a voice . . . the first is quality . . . the second is range. In most cases, it is the quality which is the more important factor. A voice sounds "like a soprano" even though it may be singing low tones. Another voice has the quality of an alto even though the singer may sing quite high.

Listed below are the approximate ranges for various voices. These are "average ranges" . . . there are individuals who sing higher and lower than the ranges given yet their voices are classified within these divisions.

LYRIC SOPRANO   MEZZO SOPRANO   CONTRALTO   TENOR   BARITONE   BASS

Questions:

1. Which is more important in determining classification of a voice, the range or the quality? _____.

2. Name the two classifications for girls' voices. _____, _____.

3. In this country we believe that the boy (should sing) (should not sing) while his voice is changing. (Cross out one.)

4. Voices usually change when a boy is in his early _____.

5. What is the highest voice called? _____. What is the lowest voice called? _____.

Quality of Voices

As we learned in the previous lesson, the quality of the voice is most important in deciding upon the part we are to sing.

The soprano voices are classified as LYRIC... (a light, high, flute-like quality), DRAMATIC (heavy quality), COLORATURA (voice which has flexibility and can sing trills, fast passages), and the most common of all the MEZZO-SOPRANO voice. Actually MEZZO means (half) and this voice, like the baritone of the men's voices, is between the highest and lowest classifications. Most girl singers have mezzo-soprano quality.

In a girls' trio we should have a lyric soprano, mezzo-soprano, and alto. In most of our thinking, the words alto and contralto mean the same thing.

The tenor voices are classified as LYRIC (light), DRAMATIC (heavy); while the baritones and the basses round out the picture.

Many young singers have an idea that they would like to sing some special part. "I want to be a soprano" has been stated by many girls joining the school choir. Yet this is NOT the correct attitude. We sing with the voice which we have. We might wish to change our voices, and we might make SOME changes in this way, but we cannot hope to change our classification merely by wishing.

Each of us has been given a vocal instrument which is US. We can improve it, we can learn to use it correctly, but we cannot expect to sing some part with a quality which we do not have and a range which we do not have. To have a good choir requires that each of the voices be singing on the part where they belong. This is most important.

In chorus singing we have many different arrangements of the same song. For example: it may be published for girls' choirs— 2-parts, 3-parts, 4-parts (occasionally); mixed choirs: 3 parts SAB, or 4 parts SATB; and boys' choir: usually 4 parts TTBB. With such a fine variety, it is true that almost every song is published within the range of all of the voices so that each of us may sing within our proper voice classification.

Here is the proper listing of an 8-part chorus from the highest voices down: Lyric soprano, dramatic soprano, mezzo-soprano, alto, lyric tenor, dramatic tenor, baritone, bass.

Questions:

1. Which classification enrolls the largest number of girls? _____.

2. Which classification enrolls the largest number of boys? _____.

3. Name the soprano voice which is most flexible. _____.

4. What word means about the same as alto? _____.

5. Should we expect to sing the part we wish, or the part we are qualified to sing?

_____ _____ _____.

Resonance

As we learned when we first discussed the singing process, the breath passes over the vocal cords and produces a tone. This is reenforced in our resonance cavities and as it passes out of our mouth and nose, the tones and words are formed. While we have resonance without being conscious of it, we should spend a few lessons in discussing resonance so that each singer will understand something about it.

There are, in the body, 3 air chambers which are directly connected with the singing process. These are the chest, the mouth, and the nose. In some books the nose is called the head.

If we were to take a violin string and stretch it over a string bass, we would not have the sound of a violin OR of a bass. The string would be tuned too high to set the maximum response from the air inside of the bass. High tones need a small amount of resonance area. Lower tones need more space.

It may be possible that you have a tuning bar in your school. If you cover up the opening (under the bar) and then strike the bar, you will discover that you have a very soft tone. When you remove the cover ... and allow the tones to be reenforced in the resonance cavity under the bar, you get a much larger and richer sound.

The same is true in our voices. One will hear a very sweet voice ... but so soft and tiny that one can hardly hear it. With the proper reenforcement of a tone ... the voice will sound much larger.

In each voice, the chest should reenforce the lowest tones ... the mouth will have to reenforce all tones or else there will be no words ... and the head (nasal pharynx) will reenforce the high tones.

As we have stated before, when we sing our highest tones, it may be impossible for us to say words. Perhaps the tones are reenforced in our head to the point that the mouth cavity does not enter into the picture as it should. If we place our hand on our chest ... (below the breastbone) we will feel vibrations when we sing our lowest tones. By the same token, if we press our fingers against the side of our nose and sing high tones, we will feel the vibrations there. While this may not help us to sing, it is interesting to see how the human body follows the laws of acoustics in resonance as well as vibration.

Questions:

1. Resonance is _____ of a tone.

2. Name the three resonance cavities of the human voice. _____, _____, _____.

3. Most resonance for a low tone would come from the _____.

4. What resonance enters all tones if we are to have words? _____.

5. Does the human voice follow the laws of acoustics? _____.

Registers

In the chart below we have, in a crude way, shown how the various resonance cavities reenforce the tones. Notice that the mouth is found in ALL singing or else we do not have words ... that as we sing higher the head resonance is added GRADUALLY.

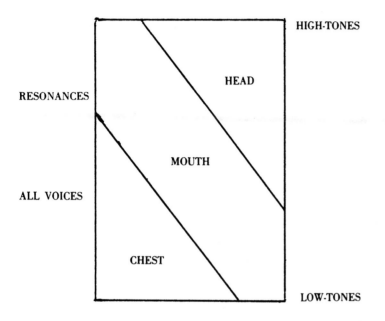

By an improper use of resonances, some voices have noticeable breaks. The break is usually not caused by the vibrating of our vocal cords ... but by our changing of resonances. The cure for the break in any voice is to vocalize downward from medium high tones. When we vocalize downward the break is usually eliminated. We then vocalize upward trying to make the tones the same as when we came down. Do not change the position of the singing organs. ...

Because of this break, some teachers have used the word register. We are singing in our chest register, our head register, etc. In this case, the word register has a similar meaning to resonance.

Actually, each of us should be able to sing our entire range with little change in quality. Any changes which do take place should be gradual and not abrupt. We do not wish to hear a change of quality ... or a change in color. As the lyric soprano and tenor voices sing higher, the quality gradually gets lighter. As they sing lower they lose their brilliance and they can hardly be heard. As the alto and baritone or bass voices sing higher, the tones get richer, louder (usually), and more resonant. As these voices sing lower the same rich quality continues.

Each of us should practice to have the same rich sounds throughout the entire range of our voices ... from our lowest to our highest singing notes. There should not be any breaks in our voices.

Questions:

1. What is the recommended cure for a break in the voice? _____ _____.

2. What word has a similar meaning to register? _____.

3. Changes in quality in any voice should be made _____.

4. As a lyric tenor sings higher the voice gets _____.

5. As an alto sings higher the voice gets _____ _____.

Reading Music

One of the most important phases of music is the ability to read notation. This is extremely important to both the vocalist and the instrumentalist. Reading instrumentally is much different than reading vocally. No matter what key we may be playing, the fingering of most instruments remains the same. Instrumentalists use a system of "fixed DO". Vocally, we are not so fortunate.

In choral music, we sing tones which sound "in relation to other tones." Any sound we may sing may be called by any syllable name. We have a "movable DO" and are able to sing in keys with different key signatures with equal ease.

Instrumentalists usually spend months and even years before being eligible to belong to a band or an orchestra. Vocalists, on the other hand, are able to sing in choirs without receiving any musical instruction. Membership in a choir may enable the singer to learn to read simple melodies without ever receiving a private or a class lesson.

Instruments have become standardized. No matter what cornet we may play, we expect that the fingering for certain tones will be the same. In voice, we are working with an "unseen" instrument . . . and all an individual can do is suggest that we produce certain effects. The actual singing comes from within the singer himself.

This should convince us that reading music vocally is NOT an easy task. Some of our better known singers are very poor music readers. Some of our "pop" singers openly admit that they do not know how to read music. Some singers, who never sing professionally at all, are very fine readers.

There is a music talent which is known as "absolute pitch". There are quite a few individuals who can recognize the sound which they hear and give it its true name. For instance a person hearing the squeaking of a car brake might say, "that sounds like a D", and it would have been a "D".

With practice, many singers can learn to recognize sounds which they hear. It is but a short step to reverse the process and to sing the tone which they see. Entire school choirs have been taught to "take the pitch" because it "sounds right." In most school choirs there are individuals who have such a fine sense of pitch that they can lead the various voice sections. While it is a great help to sing with piano accompaniment, it is a most difficult experience when the piano is out of tune.

Because reading music is so important to the singer, it is recommended that each singer try and develop a good sense of pitch. Keep trying to guess what the next pitch is to be and in a short time it will be amazing to see how close the "guessing" will become.

Questions:

1. We use a fixed "DO" with _____ music.

2. When we sing, we use a _____ "DO".

3. Is it easier to read instrumental or choral music? _____.

4. Some people are able to name the sounds they hear. This is called _____ _____.

5. Some professional singers are _____ to read music.

Reading by Interval

In his high school and college music program, the serious student deals with musical intervals. An interval is the amount of tonal distance between two tones. Intervals may be the notes in a chord . . . or they may be the distance between tones in a melody.

When we sing a tone, we should "fix" the sound in our minds. When we return to it, it will have the same sound. For instance, when we sing SWANEE RIVER . . . we fix in our minds the first sound "Way" . . . and a second later we are singing the same pitch on "On". In other words, the tone is the same for the following underlined words . . . "*Way* down up-*on* the Swanee River."

Let us look for a moment at this familiar melody. We find that the second phrase is almost exactly the same as the first. We find that the music follows a scale line . . . or it follows a chord which we recognize. By guessing the interval higher or lower which we must sing, we "come close" to singing the right tones.

(Of course, this is not accurate singing, but it is the way that most individuals sing. In the following lesson we shall learn about a more accurate way of singing.)

Notice that measures 5 and 1 are the same, 6 and 2 are the same, 7 is quite like 3. Measure 3 is built on the Tonic Chord which is the chord that might be given before the song starts.

Starting with the first sound, notice that we then move down the scale, then up to the word "ON" and again down the scale. On the big interval jump . . . "Swa-nee" this is an octave . . . it is a full scale higher. Etc.

By thinking about the tones which we have sung . . . and may return to; and by thinking about the next tone . . . higher or lower . . . scalewise or with a jump, we are able to improve our music reading.

Like learning to skate, one must spend considerable time before one is able to "travel on his own" . . . in reading music. However, with experience one is able to get some idea of what is coming next. Experience should improve the reading ability of any singer.

Questions:

1. Select some song and discuss the scalewise and chordwise progressions which we find.

Syllables

Several hundreds of years ago, a church musician by the name of Guido invented a system of music reading which we call Solfeggio. Using the first syllables of a Latin Chant, he named each of the tones of a scale. As the word "scale" indicates a ladder, so the tones of the scale ascend in steps and half steps. Starting on middle "C" on the piano, and playing the white keys in order upward, we have the syllable names

DO, RAY, ME, FAH, SO, LAH, TEE, DO.
(Written Do, Re, Mi, Fa, Sol, La, Ti, Do)

We should notice in this exercise that we have all of the five prime vowels represented. (AYE- Ray; EEH- ME; AH- FAH; OH- SO; OOH- DO — if you call it DO). (Some teachers call DO- DOH. Others call it DO as in the sentence "I can do it.")

In playing up the scale, we find that we have black keys between all of the tones except Mi-Fa; Ti-Do. In other words, we have whole step intervals between all of the tones of the scale except 3-4, 7-8. This is true of any major scale. We may sing our syllables starting on any tone . . . C-sharp, D, E-flat or any other . . . and the syllables have the same relationship each to the other no matter what the key.

In most of our schools some form of music reading is started in the early grades. Some schools use numbers in which each of the tones of the scale are named 1, 2, 3, etc. Others (a smaller number) call the tones by their names (lines and spaces of the staff). The largest number of schools teach music reading by syllables. By the time that students are in the sixth or seventh grade they will probably have acquired most of the ability to read music they will ever have. When music was first introduced into our schools, music reading was one of the major objectives. Today reading music is shared with ability to sing, play an instrument, create music (write music), listen to music, and know facts about music. Because so few people used music reading in their adult lives, music programs in school offered more "lasting" phases of music.

In addition to the syllable names of the major scale, there are also syllables which cover the half steps (the black keys).

Because few individuals read music by syllables, and because most choirs do not, we are not spending more time on the subject of music reading. While music reading is most important to every musician, the subject is so broad that it must of necessity be treated in a separate course.

Questions:

1. What is the fourth syllable of the scale? _____ the seventh? _____.

2. What was the name of the inventor of syllables? _____.

3. What is the name given to syllable singing? _____.

4. What are other ways of teaching music reading besides syllables?

_____ _____ _____ _____.

5. Where were the names of the syllables found? _____

Interpretation

Music is one of the greatest of art forms. The music which one sings may have been written hundreds of years ago... or it may have been written but a few moments ago. It is the task of the singer to perform the music as the composer intended. This is not an easy assignment.

A great deal has been written about feeling the "mood" of a song. If the composer gave us a fine composition, then the words and the music UNITE to tell a story ... to paint a picture. The words and the music are equally important. Each adds to the beauty of the other. Interpretation means that we have an understanding of the "message of the song" and that we pass this along to our listeners.

In order to properly interpret a song, we should first study the text ... the words. If we do not know what the words mean, then we must look them up in a dictionary. We study the stanzas of the lyrics (the poem). We decide where we will take our breath, and where we will phrase our singing. If we are to get across the meaning of the words, we must speak them so that the listener will understand each one of them. After we are certain that we know what the words are telling us, we turn to the music.

This should be in keeping with the mood which the words have set. If we are singing about something sad

... we expect that the melody and the harmony will help us establish this mood. The introduction of the song sets the mood for us even before we sing. We must be "in the mood" of the composition ... and even after it is over and we are taking a bow ... we are still in that mood which we have created through the music we have sung.

Young singers are often guilty of singing songs which have little meaning to them. Small children can have little personal understanding of some of the deeply religious songs which one hears them trying to sing. As the Scripture states ... "When I was a child, I understood as a child".... There are many fine songs within the understanding of every singer and we should limit ourselves to these. There was once a very small lad who sang ... "Darling I Am Growing Old ... Silver Threads Among the Gold". As he finished, he turned to the little girl beside him and whispered "Wait until I grow up".

Because so many songs have a definite style, tempo (speed), and a standard interpretation, it is wise for the young singer to listen to a fine recording made by some recognized singer. Although it is possible that even these may not be accurate, it is quite likely that the over-all effect will be in keeping with the wishes of the composer.

Questions:

1. It is the task of the singer to perform the music the way the _____ intended.

2. The words and the music unite to give a _____.

3. In learning a song, we should first study the _____.

4. Words in a song are called _____.

5. In order to be sure of our interpretation, we should _____ _____ _____ _____.

Elements of Music

For one to interpret correctly, one must be able to read the notation ... to know the terminology.

Briefly we shall consider what the composer has to give us. For more detailed information, the study of various books dealing with Music Theory is necessary.

All sounds in the world have been divided into noises and tones. Music deals with tones. Each tone has four characteristics: it is high or low, (pitch); loud or soft (intensity or volume); long or short (duration); and it has a quality which may be different from other tones (timbre).

Through the notation, the composer gives us an idea of each of these four qualities of a tone. Through the position of notes on the staff and the clef which he uses, we have pitch and duration given. Through tempo words such as presto (fast), largo (slow), we have a rate of speed indicated. With a metronome indication, we can

have an absolute speed given us. Then we may have faster (accel.) or slower (rit.) indicated.

Intensity is shown by letters (FF—very loud, PP—very soft) and we have other words which show louder and softer ... (cres ... dim).

Quality can only be suggested ... accented, sweetly, like a march, etc.

The singer will find that after studying the words to get their meaning, and learning the proper notation, he will then wish to study the music to learn the tempo and dynamics which the composer intended. Notice these things as you listen to the recording of the song which you are studying. Does the artist follow the suggestions which the composer has given? If not, does it add or detract from the mood which the composer wanted to set?

Sooner or later one is faced with the problem of

"singing the song the way he feels it." This is all very fine and each person gives a bit of himself in every song he sings, but be sure that your own wishes are similar to those of the composer. After all ... it is the composer's song ... and we are allowed to enjoy singing it. We always try and present the music as the composer intended.

Listening to several different recordings of orchestras playing the same number, we find that each conductor takes certain "liberties" with the music ... but we also find that by and large, it is pretty much alike ... no matter what orchestra may play it. The same is true of singers. If we sing a selection correctly, it will sound similar to the singing of the same selection by others.

Study the words, the music, and listen to your teacher's interpretation ... then add a few suggestions of your own ... all in the mood of the selection being sung.

Questions:

1. Name the two classes of sounds. _____ , _____ .

2. What is the word meaning high or low? _____ .

3. What does intensity mean? _____ .

4. What does long or short indicate? _____ .

5. Give a word which means the same as quality. _____ .

LESSON 38   # Foreign Language Songs

Many of our great vocal composers did not write their songs in English. If we are to sing their songs, we either sing a translation of the lyrics they wrote, or we sing the song using a foreign language.

At this point we would like to voice a warning. Many young singers in our high schools believe that to sing a foreign-language song adds to their prestige as a singer. This may be true to amateur listeners; it is not true to the trained vocalist. Poor pronunciation, and sloppy enunciation cannot be excused merely because one sings in a foreign language. There are still the same fundamentals of good speech which we must expect. We still sing on the vowels with consonants forming the words. Phrases must be kept intact ... we do not take a breath in the middle of a word, even though it is a foreign word.

In singing foreign-language songs, which every serious singer will eventually do, we should first study the translation of the words. Let us know what we are singing! How can we interpret the song ... give it meaning to ourselves and our listeners, when we do not know what it is saying? After we have absorbed the meaning, after we understand each word of the song, we then learn to speak the words correctly. In this respect we again turn to a fine teacher or we turn to a recording. Notice every syllable ... the inflection of the voice ... and as we learn the pronunciation ... associate the meaning of the word to the sounds we are making.

While it is true that many of the great art songs have been written in foreign languages, we must not overlook the many fine songs which we also have in English. Young singers in this country should sing almost all of their songs in their own language. A lovely voice does not need to "impress" an audience with singing a foreign-language song. However, if you do sing such a song, be sure that you sing it correctly ... and that in some way you let the audience know the story of the song you are singing.

It is in poor taste to visit a friend's home and then speak in a language which he will not understand. It is equally poor to sing for an audience in a language which it does not understand ... unless a translation is given on the program or unless you explain the meaning of the selection.

Many young singers in music festivals have tried to impress the judges by their singing of a foreign-language song only to learn that their pronunciation was faulty, that they did not interpret the song correctly, and when asked to explain of what they were singing, found it had practically no meaning to them.

By all means sing foreign-language songs because much of our fine choral literature came from these peoples, but be certain that you understand of what you are singing ... and also be sure that your audience knows what you are singing.

Questions:

1. In singing a foreign-language song, we should first study the _____

2. Why do we have to sing foreign-language songs? _____ .

3. Name 3 things to consider in good singing of foreign-language songs.

    a. _____ .

    b. _____   c. _____

Tessitura

It is most important that each singer select a song which is within the range of his voice. If we visit a music store and ask for a copy of some standard work, the clerk will ask us whether we wish it in a high key, a medium key, or a low key. Some popular vocal solos are provided in five or six different keys. This is to help us find a key which is best suited to our voice.

But in the selection of a solo, it is not only a question of how high or how low we have to sing, but also of the number of times we have to sing these high and low tones. As we found out in Lesson 27, we are able to vocalize, on staccato exercises, much higher than we would dare sing in public. So, in selecting a song which is within the range of our voices, we avoid singing our highest and our lowest tones until we are certain that we can always sing them.

Tessitura is a word which means "the way in which the song lies for our voices". It is high, or medium, or low. It fits our voice and we can sing it with comfort and ease.

As we learned in Lesson 29, when a boy's voice is changing he is able to sing in a limited range. Even in this limited range, we have music which has been written especially for this purpose. Choral arrangements which are written for soprano, soprano alto, and baritone (SSAB) and some written for soprano, alto, baritone (SAB) are in this classification. One song, a solo titled the MONOTONE, uses the same note throughout the entire composition.

Typical of some of the fine songs written for a limited range, we are going to consider the melody of a famous Spiritual . . . I GOT SHOES. Notice that it has a range of only 6 tones.

I GOT SHOES.

I GOT SHOES
Spiritual

I got shoes, you got shoes, All God's chil-dren got shoes.

When I get to heav'n I'm goin' to put on my shoes.__ Goin' to

walk all ov-er God's heav'n, heav'n, heav'n,

Ev-'ry-bod-y talk-in' 'bout heav'n ain't a-goin'__ to

heav'n,__ heav'n,__ Goin' to walk all ov-er God's heav'n.

Selecting Songs

As we have learned in the previous lesson, it is most important that each singer select a song which has the correct tessitura. Because of differing interests, singers do not all prefer the same type of song.

Most music has been classified according to difficulty. There are usually three classifications: easy, medium, and difficult. The young singer should realize that there is no great reward for singing a difficult song unless it is well sung. With hundreds of titles found in each division, one should be able to select a song within his capacity.

Then, as we have stated previously, most songs are available in high, medium, or low range. Singers with extremely low voices may find that the high song, sung an octave lower than it is written, may be ideal.

Roughly all songs are divided into sacred or secular areas. Among the secular; one may find popular songs, songs from operas, songs from musical comedies, ballads (which tell a story), folk songs (our land as well as others), humorous songs, serenades, art songs, songs from various secular cantatas, and other types.

In the sacred category, one finds sacred anthems, sacred solos, hymns, motets, selections from masses, from oratorios, from cantatas, spirituals (Negro and white), and other types.

Because many of the great composers have given us songs as well as instrumental music, one may wish to sing music of the Classical period (Bach, Beethoven, Mozart, Handel, Haydn, etc.); of the Romantic period (Schubert, Schumann, Mendelssohn, Rubinstein, etc.); of the Modern period (Hindemith, Menotti, etc.).

Then one is able to sing songs from various countries. Grieg-Norway, Britten-English, Brahms-Germany, Sibelius-Finland, Schubert-Germany, Gershwin-America, Tschaikowsky-Russia, Verdi-Italy, Puccini-Italy, etc. The list seems unending.

One of the most important phases of correct singing is to select a song which is within the range of the singer . . . a song which fits his type and temperament. With such a wide selection from which to choose, any singer should find it easy to get the proper selection.

Questions:

1. There are _____ general classification of songs as to range.

2. All songs are divided into 2 types: _____ and _____.

3. The three periods of composition mentioned are: _____ _____ _____ _____.

4. List composers (not mentioned above) which are representative of the music of their country.

Stage Technic

When singing in public, one must know how to act. There are three phases to be considered: entering the stage, what to do while on the stage, and leaving the stage.

The laws of courtesy hold at all times. If two men are entering the stage, the singer enters first followed by the accompanist. The singer moves to his position near the piano (in the "bow" of the grand piano). The accompanist seats himself at the piano. When all is ready the singer gives a slight nod to the accompanist and the introduction begins.

If one of the individuals entering the stage is a lady, she enters first and at the conclusion, she will leave first. This is true whether she be the singer or the accompanist.

If two women are entering the stage, the singer precedes the accompanist.

Before singing a selection, pause a moment and "get the mood" in your mind. Think of the message of your song. From the moment the accompaniment starts, you are in that mood. Stay in the mood until the last note has been performed . . . soloist or accompaniment. Hold the mood until the very conclusion of the selection.

There is always the question of applause. It is proper that the audience should applaud when the singer enters the stage. This may not happen. In this case, the singer merely goes to his place . . . nods to the accompanist

. . . and sings. If there is applause, advance to your position . . . then take a bow, acknowledging the applause. After the selection is finished, take a bow . . . and wait until the applause has ended before getting into the mood of the next selection.

The young singer should practice taking a bow before appearing in public. It is good to have someone watch you and make suggestions. It is easy to bow when we bow from the waist . . . not too stiff and rigid . . . keep head down and don't watch the audience while bowing. Some singers find it more informal to merely bend the head in a slight motion and smile. Some singers will bow slightly and whisper the words "thank you."

Some singers like to say a few words to the audience . . . explaining the song they are going to sing. This may be fine in the case of a foreign-language song. It is relaxing to the singer . . . less formal than otherwise.

There is the matter of singing an encore. If the singer believes that the audience has enjoyed the song and would like to hear another, then the encore should be ready. Don't wait too long . . . the applause may have died down and some of the listeners may be leaving the auditorium. After singing a solo program, it is proper to have an encore or two (usually of the novelty nature) to sing at the close of the program. Send your audience away with a "song on their lips and in their hearts".

Questions:

1. Before singing, the soloist should pause and "_____".

2. When two men enter the stage the _____ enters first.

3. When a man and a women enter the stage the _____ enters first.

4. The singer should remain in the mood of his song until after _____ _____.

5. Why should an encore be sung before waiting too long? _____ _____ _____.

Singing in Choirs

Singing alone may give us great pleasure, but singing in groups opens up "another world" of choral enjoyment. Now we hear the blending of voices, the balance of parts. Here is choral harmony.

Most communities present greater opportunities for group singing than for solo singing. This is found in churches, schools, community choirs, etc.

A few centuries ago the most popular small ensembles of singers were called MADRIGAL SINGERS. There were usually five, six, or seven singers, seated about a table ... usually one person singing each part. There were many combinations of singers: women, men, and mixed voices. Today there are many madrigal groups in our country ... in schools, colleges, and adult organizations.

To sing in a madrigal ensemble, one must be a good reader, able to hold his own part ... in other words, a fine choral musician. With no piano accompaniment, and with no one to help you "find your own part", it is necessary that you be a fine musician to participate in this, one of the highest forms of the vocalist's art.

Large ensembles are called choirs. Like the madrigals, these may be composed of women alone (SSA music — soprano, 2nd soprano, alto), composed of men alone (TTBB — Tenor, tenor, baritone, bass); or mixed voices (SATB, SSAATTBB, etc.)

Singing in a choir is different than singing alone. Here one has to follow a conductor ... he has to "sing with the others". He not only must start and stop with the others, but he must speak his words with the others. In a choir, all of the voices sing as one unit.

There are several important factors to consider in selecting voices for a choir. First is one's ability to sing the proper part ... the part to which the voice is properly classified. Then there is one's ability to blend with the other voices. One should not hear one voice "above the others". One way to get a blend of voices is to sing softly. We soften our own voice until we hear the voices of others about us. Then, one should be able to read music ... at least to equal the ability of the other singers. And finally ... one should have enough choral training so that he will contribute to the improvement of the organization.

Singers should be able to read (and sing) their proper part. Sopranos may find that the melody is usually assigned to their part ... but this is not always so. Singing solos ... we sing the melody. Singing in the choir, only a few voices may have the melody while others are singing harmony parts.

We usually start part singing in the schools at about the fourth or fifth grade. Starting this young, children are able to sing their own parts by the time they are in junior high school where, if we have changed voices in the boys, we sing SATB music of an easy grade. From senior high school on to college and adult life we have many-part choirs (SSAATTBB).

Questions:

1. In singing madrigals, we usually have _____ person on a part.

2. Give one reason for the statement that singing in a choir is different from

singing alone. _____ _____ _____.

3. Name 3 important steps to consider in accepting a person as a choir member.

 a. _____ _____ _____ _____.

 b. _____ _____ _____ _____.

 c. _____ _____ _____ _____.

A Cappella Singing

Chorus singing is of two types: accompanied or a cappella. Some music can best be sung in each of these classifications, and there are both advantages and disadvantages connected with singing either one.

In singing with accompaniment, many of the voices will learn to depend entirely upon the tones which a piano or organ may play for them. In some advanced compositions, we find that the piano and organ have different parts. Learning to depend entirely upon the accompaniment does not teach us to read as well as when we have to sing independently. However . . . when the accompaniment differs from the voices, it adds a great deal to the beauty of the selection.

A cappella singing, which was used extensively a century or two ago in the churches of the world requires that each part sing the proper tones without any "outside help". A cappella singing trains the musicians to listen to each other. While the entire choir may flat or sharp . . . they all flat and sharp together so that the chords "within the choir" are in tune with each other. Then too, singers learn to "balance the chords". They listen to see that they can hear all of the parts equally well. It would be poor a cappella singing if all one heard were the soprano or the bass parts. We must hear all parts equally balanced.

It is recommended that choirs should sing both a cappella and accompanied. Choirs which sing entirely a cappella may find that when an accompaniment is added, they sing so poorly in tune that no one wishes to hear it. On the other hand, the choir which always sings with accompaniment, may find that when asked to sing unaccompanied, the voices are unsure of themselves.

As a balanced meal consists of several different dishes of food, so the well-balanced choral program will include songs of many different types . . . a cappella and accompanied, sacred and secular.

In singing a cappella, the choir has to obtain the pitch. This may be given by a chord struck on the piano, by someone blowing a pitch pipe, by someone with "absolute pitch" giving the key tone, or by taking the pitch from the previous song. Choirs have taken pitch before entering the stage, keeping the pitch in mind until the song started. All of this is a matter of choral training which the fine choral conductor will demand and which the serious minded singer has a right to expect.

Questions:

1. Unaccompanied choral singing is called _____ _____.

2. Give one weakness of singing with an accompaniment. _____ _____ _____ _____.

3. Give one weakness of unaccompanied singing. _____ _____ _____ _____.

4. Name 3 ways a choir may take the pitch. _____ _____ _____ _____.

5. Do we have music in which the organ plays a different part than the singers sing? _____.

Accompanists

As we have seen, solo singing and much chorus singing is done with accompaniment. In many programs, the accompaniment is half of the program. We should therefore spend one lesson in considering what it takes to be a good accompanist.

1. The accompanist should be a sensitive musician. He should be skilled at playing the piano or organ to the point where he does not hold back the soloist or the choir.

2. The accompanist should have studied choral music to the point where he recognizes the difficulties which the vocalist faces. In other words, if the song goes high and the singer is giving his all to sing the tones properly, the accompanist will naturally play louder ... perhaps give the singer greater confidence by pushing the beat a little.

3. While the accompanist must be willing to assume the second place in the choral performance (the soloist is the artist-singer), the singer at the same time should recognize the accompanist ... work out the details of the selections in advance ... recognize the musicianship of the accompanist ... and in turn ... share the applause with him.

In school choirs, it is good to have more than one individual serving as accompanist. Some writers have stated that accompanists "are born with the ability to follow". We rather believe that it comes from much hard work. Playing an accompaniment for a singer over a long period of time, the accompanist learns by intuition when the singer will pause for a breath ... and when he will wish to speed up the tempo. The same is true with choral conductors. What a wonderful satisfaction it is to work with an accompanist who anticipates your interpretation of a number. If music is to be a truly great art ... the singer and the accompanist must work together as a team.

In major performances, accompaniment may be provided by an orchestra, a band, or various other instrumental combinations. In every case, the singer is the soloist and the instrumental group should be the accompaniment ... it should follow the soloist. The conductor will watch the singer for his "cues". In this case, the conductor becomes the accompanist, directing the ensemble much as the pianist plays upon the keys. Both the conductor and the singer share in the applause of the audience.

Questions:

1. What is the greatest task of the accompanist? _____ _____ _____ _____.

2. Should the accompanist study choral music? _____.

3. Name four accompaniments. _____ _____ _____ _____.

4. The singer and the accompanist must work together as a _____.

5. The accompanist should be a _____ musician.

Suggestions for Singers

In concluding our discussion of the fundamentals of singing, we wish to go over the major points which we have made.

The steps in singing are these:

We inhale . . . through our mouth and nose, breath is taken into our lungs.

We exhale . . . and breath passing over our vocal cords sets them into vibration. These vocal cords react in three different ways, they tighten, they touch or approximate, and they thicken and thin within themselves.

Tones caused by the vibration of the vocal cords are reenforced in our resonance cavities: chest, mouth, head.

Tones passing out of our mouths are changed by tongue, lips, teeth, and palate as words are formed.

The way in which we state our words gives us correct enunciation and pronunciation. Words sung together give us musical phrases and musical phrases give us the interpretation of songs.

We may start tones by gradually allowing the breath to pass over the vocal cords . . . or we may have the breath move across them with an attack which is called the stroke of the glotis. If we wish a soft attack we start the breath first. If we wish a loud, sforzando attack, we start the tone with a lot of breath support at the beginning.

We should be able to sing all tones from our highest tone to our lowest tone without changing our head position. In other words, the singing of tones comes from within us. We do not need to bow our heads for high tones or to tuck our chins against our chest for low tones.

We should not have sagging shoulders or hunched shoulders when we sing. We stand or sit erect . . . naturally. Singing is not something which makes us act in an artificial manner.

In finding ways to improve our singing, we should always take the items in the chart given above . . . the steps in singing . . . and follow them through in order. In all of this we are relaxed and not rigid.

Questions:

Name 5 steps which we follow when we sing.

1. _____.

2. _____.

3. _____.

4. _____.

5. _____.

Common Faults of Singers

It is seldom that we find perfection in any art form. There are few singers who sing perfectly and few choirs which ever sing an anthem without some voices doing incorrect things. However . . . we work TOWARD PERFECTION. We try to improve our singing: individually and in groups. To help us check ourselves and others we may hear sing, we have listed some of the common faults of singers.

FAULTS WE MAY HEAR
   Sharping or flatting
   Scooping on an attack
   Singing the "wrong" vowel sound
   Sliding from one vowel to another
   Trying to sing too forward or too far back
   Singing diphthongs with the emphasis on the wrong vowel
   Speaking a word incorrectly
   Taking a breath in the middle of a phrase, even in the middle of a word
   Singing incorrect pitches (especially in choirs)

   Failing to give the correct time value to tones
   Not in the "mood" of the composition
   A tight, rigid tone
   Hollow mouth tone quality
   Too heavy a vibrato . . . voice is not pure and clear
   Throaty sound
   Breathy quality
   Weak tone . . . lacks support

FAULTS WE MAY SEE
   Falling chest
   Humped shoulders
   Wrinkled forehead
   Grinning smile
   Not in mood of composition
   Sloppy appearance . . . standing or sitting
   Wrinkled nose
   Poor lip position for the vowel being sung
   Standing on toes for "high tones"
   The reader may add to this list as he observes himself and other singers.

Cures for Common Faults

Because the human voice is such a delicate instrument and we have to work through the power of suggestion, it seems as though we were setting up an "opposite fault" to cure the fault which we have observed. If a person sings flat (out of tune), we try and get them to sing sharper. If a person sings sharp, we try and get them to flat until they are singing the correct pitch. We must be careful that we do not carry these "cures" to the point where they become faults in themselves.

The suggested cures for the faults which were listed in the previous lessons are:

Trying to sing "sharper" will help cure flatting.

Trying to sing "flatter" will help cure sharping.

Short staccato exercises will tend to cure: scooping on attack, singing wrong pitches, a tight rigid sound, breathy quality.

Vocalizing on the five prime vowel sounds will tend to cure singing wrong vowel sound, sliding from one vowel to another, trying to keep the voice too forward or too far in the back of the throat, and speaking the word incorrectly.

Long sustained tones will help cure taking a breath in the middle of a phrase, tight rigid sound, too heavy a vibrato, and breathy quality.

Clear enunciation (at the front of the mouth) should correct incorrect pronunciation.

If in doubt about the emphasis being given to certain vowels of diphthongs, look up the correct pronunciation in a dictionary. Remember we speak and sing with the same pronunciation. Singing is speech on a tone.

Rigid singing is not good. We must relax our throats and our jaws...sing in a relaxed manner but with good breath support.

If our voices sound too dark...and we are singing too far in the back of our throats...try bringing the voice forward with the bright vowel sounds...EEH and AYE. If on the other hand the voice is too forward, use the dark vowels OH and OOH.

A cure for the faults which we see...is merely not to be guilty of them. Members of a voice class can help other members by pointing out things which they do which are not a part of good singing.

We should move our shoulders very little when we sing. We do not go up on our toes to sing high notes. We do not change the head position when we sing to low tones. We smile on songs which are humorous...we do not smile if the song is serious. We try to sing each word so that someone could "read our lips" and understand every word...because we have the proper formation.

Many of us make mistakes when we sing...yet the good singer makes fewer mistakes and each time we sing, we try to improve our singing by making fewer mistakes.

Questions:

1. What are your most common faults as a singer? _____ _____ _____ _____

_____ _____ _____ _____ _____ _____

_____ _____ _____ _____ _____ _____

2. What do you recommend as cures for your faults? _____ _____ _____ _____

_____ _____ _____ _____ _____ _____ _____

_____ _____ _____

Knowing Our Own Voices

As we vocalize, we shall probably find that one or more vowel sounds seem to be "our best." Perhaps we hear our teacher say: "that is it . . . there is the sound I have been waiting for." This is the tone which represents our best vocal effort. If we can remember the "sound" of this tone, it will help us improve our singing. Every time we sing we try and sound "like it."

As we learned in an early lesson, we sing on five prime vowels. In the chart below we have listed these vowels . . . and we have given a range on which we can record our own voice. We check the sounds we sing well in keeping with the vowels we sing and the tones on which we sing them. As we continue our study we will improve our singing. We shall be able to sing more vowel sounds "well" and we shall extend our range higher and lower. The chart will aid us in improving our singing.

GIRLS VOICES

EEH

AYE

AH

OH

OOH

BOYS VOICES

The following is an example of a high school baritone's range.

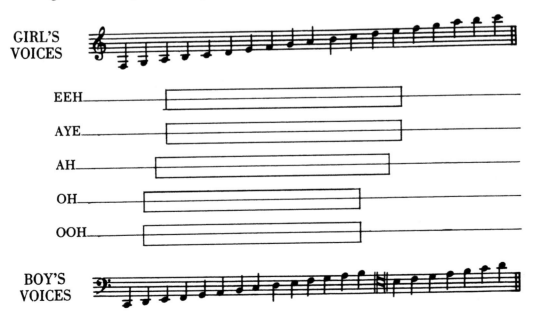

Everyone Sings

In our land everyone sings. We sing in our homes, in our churches, in our fraternal organizations, in our schools. We have millions of people who sing every week.

In the preceding lessons we have discussed the fundamentals of singing in a language which we can understand. There is nothing magic about singing . . . for each of us can learn to sing correctly which after all, is the best singing that we can do. Most of us do not intend to become professional singers, yet each of us can sing correctly and enjoy every opportunity we may have for singing.

In the popular field there are those singers who through some "style of singing" acquire great popularity. On the other hand, we have the more "permanent" type of singer who sings correctly and depends upon the beauty of his singing rather than some "style" to continue his popularity.

Some of the fine popular choirs which we hear on radio and television are examples of the finest in singing. As we watch them (and listen to them sing), we are now able to notice the correct vowel sounds we hear . . . the fine articulation of their words. We notice how they phrase a song . . . where they breathe and where they carry over a phrase.

In the concert field we hear fine artists. We purchase their recordings because we enjoy beautiful voices singing songs correctly. EVERYONE SINGS has opened up a new door of enjoyment for us because we have learned not only to improve our own singing but we have also learned to evaluate other people's singing and to appreciate the finer points of singing.

America is a great singing nation . . . and throughout our lives we will be doing our bit to improve our standards of choral music . . . be it in singing solo, in singing in small ensembles, or singing in choirs.